Sly Fox
Little Red Hen

Retold by Jenny Giles   Illustrated by Isabel Lowe

NELSON PRICE MILBURN

Once upon a time,
Sly Fox lived with his old mother
deep within a forest.
For a long time,
Sly Fox had been trying to catch
Little Red Hen.

Little Red Hen lived in a house
up in a tree.
Whenever she went out,
Sly Fox would watch her and follow her,
but he could not catch her.
She was always too quick for him.

Then one day,
Sly Fox thought of a way
to catch Little Red Hen.

He said to his old mother,
"Put the pot on to boil.
I will bring Little Red Hen
home for supper tonight, Mother."

And Sly Fox set off
through the forest with a sack
over his shoulder.

5

When Sly Fox reached the tree
where Little Red Hen lived,
he sat, and watched, and waited...

At last, Little Red Hen
came out of her house.
She went down to the pond
to get some water.
As quick as a flash,
Sly Fox jumped up the tree,
and disappeared into
Little Red Hen's house.

7

But when Little Red Hen
went back into her house,
she caught sight of a bushy tail.
"Oh, no!" she said to herself.
"Sly Fox is here in my house!"
She flew straight up
to her high perch.

9

Little Red Hen called down to Sly Fox.
"You may have found your way
into my house, Sly Fox,
but you will never be able
to reach me up here!"

"Aha!" grinned Sly Fox.
"I may not be able to reach you,
but I am still going to catch you!"

And he placed his sack on the floor,
right under Little Red Hen.

Peas Wheat Worms Snails

Sly Fox began to run
round the sack.
Little Red Hen sat and watched him.
Round and round the sack
ran Sly Fox...
round and round and round.

As Little Red Hen watched Sly Fox,
her head went round and round, too.
She became dizzier and dizzier.
Soon she was so dizzy
that she lost her balance.
Down she fell...
right into Sly Fox's sack!

Laughing with glee,
Sly Fox picked up the sack
and put it over his shoulder.
Then he jumped down from the tree
and ran into the forest.

But Little Red Hen was heavy,
and Sly Fox grew tired.
He stopped to rest,
and put the sack down
by a small pile of stones.
He lay back, and soon
he was fast asleep.

Little Red Hen found a tiny hole
in the sack,
and she peeped through it.
She could see that Sly Fox was asleep.
So, very carefully,
she crept out of the sack.

Then she noticed the stones,
and she smiled to herself.
"It is my turn to trick Sly Fox!"
she said to herself.
Little Red Hen picked up
some of the stones
and put them into the sack.

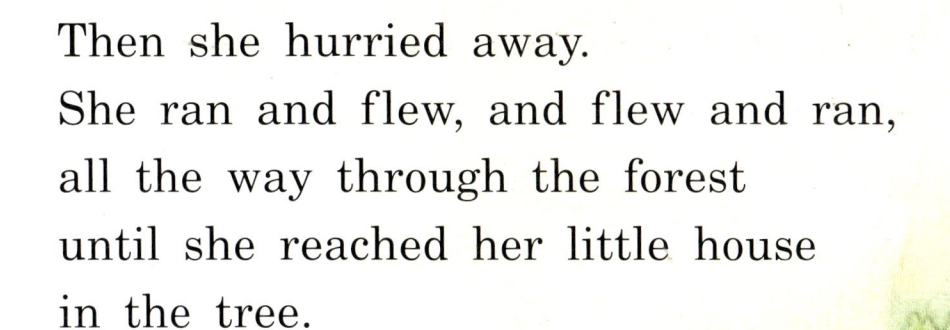

Then she hurried away.
She ran and flew, and flew and ran,
all the way through the forest
until she reached her little house
in the tree.

After a while, Sly Fox woke up.
He picked up the sack
and ran all the way home with it.
"Is the pot boiling?" he asked.
"We are having Little Red Hen
for supper tonight, just as I promised."

"The pot is ready!" said his old mother,
and she helped Sly Fox
to lift up the sack and empty it
into the boiling water.

19

With a great splash,
the stones fell into the pot.
The boiling water went all over Sly Fox
and his old mother,
and that was the end of them!

So Little Red Hen
lived happily ever after,
safe in her house up in the tree.

A play
Sly Fox and *Little Red Hen*

People in the play

Reader

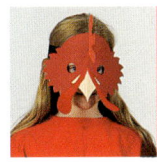

Little Red Hen

Sly Fox

Sly Fox's Mother

Reader

Once upon a time,
Sly Fox lived with his old mother
deep within a forest.
For a long time,
Sly Fox had been trying to catch
Little Red Hen.

Sly Fox

I can see Little Red Hen
up in her house in the tree.
When she comes out,
I will catch her.

Reader

So Sly Fox watched Little Red Hen,
and he followed her,
but he could not catch her.

Little Red Hen
Sly Fox will never catch me.
I am always too quick for him.

Reader
Then one day, Sly Fox thought
of a way to catch Little Red Hen.

Sly Fox
Mother, put the pot on to boil.
I will bring Little Red Hen
home for supper tonight.

Sly Fox's Mother
I shall light the fire now.

Reader
Sly Fox set off through the forest
with a sack over his shoulder.

Sly Fox

Aha!   Here is Little Red Hen's house.
I will wait for her to come out.

Reader

At last, Little Red Hen
came out of her house.

Little Red Hen

I must go down to the pond
to get some water.

Sly Fox

I will get into Little Red Hen's house
while she is down at the pond.
Then, when she comes back,
I will catch her.

Reader

But when Little Red Hen
went back into her house,
she caught sight of a bushy tail.

Little Red Hen

Oh, no! Sly Fox is here in my house.
I will fly up to my perch
where I will be safe.

Reader

Little Red Hen sat on her high perch
and called down to Sly Fox.

Little Red Hen

You may have found your way
into my house, Sly Fox,
but you will never be able
to reach me up here!

Sly Fox

Aha! I may not be able to reach you, but I am still going to catch you!

Reader

Sly Fox placed his sack on the floor, right under Little Red Hen.

Sly Fox (whispering)

Now I am going to run
round and round the sack.

Little Red Hen

Sly Fox has put a sack
down on my floor,
and he is running
round and round it.
I will sit up here and watch him.

Reader

As Little Red Hen watched Sly Fox,
her head went round and round, too.

Little Red Hen

I am getting dizzy
watching Sly Fox running
round and round.
Oh, I am getting dizzier and dizzier!

Reader

Soon Little Red Hen was so dizzy
that she lost her balance.
Down she fell...
right into Sly Fox's sack!

Sly Fox

Ha! Ha! Ha! I have caught
Little Red Hen at last!

Reader

Sly Fox picked up the sack
and put it over his shoulder.
Then he jumped down from the tree
and ran into the forest.

Sly Fox

Little Red Hen is very heavy!
I will have to stop for a rest.

Reader

Sly Fox put the sack down
by a small pile of stones.
He lay back, and soon he was fast asleep.

Little Red Hen

Here is a tiny hole in the sack.
I will peep through it.
Oh! I can see Sly Fox, and he is asleep.

Reader

So, very carefully, Little Red Hen
crept out of the sack.
Then she noticed the stones,
and she smiled to herself.

Little Red Hen

It is my turn to trick Sly Fox!
I will pick up some of these stones
and put them into the sack.
Then I will hurry home.

Reader

Little Red Hen ran and flew,
and flew and ran,
all the way through the forest
until she reached her little house
in the tree.

Sly Fox (waking up)

I must have fallen asleep!
I will hurry home now
because the pot will be boiling.

Reader

Sly Fox picked up the sack
and ran all the way home with it.

Sly Fox

Mother, is the pot boiling?
We are having Little Red Hen
for supper tonight, just as I promised.
She is here in my sack,
and she is very heavy.

Sly Fox's Mother
I will help you to lift her up. Come on!
Let's throw her into the pot.
The water is boiling.

Reader
Sly Fox and his mother
lifted up the sack.
With a great splash,
the stones fell into the pot.
The boiling water went all over Sly Fox
and his old mother,
and that was the end of them!

So Little Red Hen
lived happily ever after,
safe in her house up in the tree.

32